THE AMOS SHIFT

THE AMOS SHIFT

12 Mind*Shifts*

to Level Up Your Life*!*

GEORGE AMOS, JR.

JAGWEAR™
PUBLISHING

The Amos Shift. Copyright © 2020 by George Amos, Jr. All rights reserved. Printed in the United States of America. No part of this book may be used or reproduced in any manner whatsoever without written permission, except in the case of brief quotations embodied in critical articles and reviews. For more information, address Jag Wear Publishing, 1500 Wilson Way, Suite 215, Smyrna, GA 30082; info@theamosshift.com.

FIRST EDITION
Designed by www.peagreenpublishing.com
Edited by Anita Minniefield | Uneed2write@gmail.com
Library of Congress Number: 2019957825
ISBN 978-0-9982225-6-1
ISBN (ePub) 978-0-9982225-5-4

CONTENTS

Foreword iv
"SHIFT YOUR MINDSET" vi
Introduction: The Amos Shift 1
Shift 1: Tap into the Roots of Your Life 5
Shift 2: Study Your Name 11
Shift 3: Look Within to Lead 17
Shift 4: Celebrate Your Guiding Star 25
Shift 5: Live Redeemed 31
Shift 6: Nurture Your Relationships 35
Shift 7: Be and Become 43
Shift 8: Be a Solution 49
Shift 9: Seek Significance 55
Shift 10: Embrace Your Why 61
Shift 11: Reach for Your Destiny 67
Shift 12: Leave a Legacy 73
Epilogue 80

DEDICATION

This book is dedicated to my Dad. The One in heaven and the one on earth. The One, who saved, forgave, fortified and set me free. The One, who test, tries and sometimes troubles me. The One whose DNA resides inside of me. The One in me I don't always want to see. The One who enables me to be better than I sometimes give myself permission to be. The One who calls me to be like the One who set me free.

The One who pushes me to my destiny and shows me how to be a beloved son, brother, devoted husband, father, and friend. The One who will be with me until the very end.

The One who I am eternally grateful to, for allowing me to be a broken man who He put back together to bring honor to my family. The One to whom I give glory to by remembering that because of a Son, we all can be free, forgiven, and whole to walk through life, giving love to <u>all</u> those who we think deserve it the least, but need it the most.

ACKNOWLEDGEMENTS

Family is everything to me. Von, thank you for faithfully standing by me and cheering me on every step of the way. Sha'Kyra, Mia, and George III, my legacy lives on in you. George Sr. and my Mom in heaven, thank you for giving me life and instilling in me the will to be more. The Amos Clan, Johnny, Dorothy, Kathy, Patricia, Leon, Paul, Eddie and Yolanda – I love you more than you know. Lastly, Terry and Kathy your friendship has made me better. I honor you and consider you family.

Bishop Bronner, Dr. Nina, Pastors Dennis, Colleen, Tony and Kim, my life took on greater meaning when I met you. Thank you for being leaders that are real, transparent and touchable. My entire Word of Faith Family, with a special shout out to Pastor Chris, Lamonte, Archie and Dr. Trina.

To my Computer Cabling of Georgia team, Vanessa, Jessica, Sue, and Carmina, thank you for your beyond measure support throughout the years. Annette and Barry, I thank you for believing in me. Nancy McTaggart, your spirit lives within me. I will never forget how you believed in me when I was learning how to believe in myself. Lastly, Paula Palmer Green, thank you for helping me cast my vision - you rock.

FOREWORD

by
Bishop Dale C. Bronner

In order to change from where you are, you must decide where you would rather be. What does your ideal life look like? Where do you see yourself ten years down the road? How have you changed over the past ten years?

Change is the only constant in life; it is inevitable. But growth is optional. You must choose to grow and develop. Growth is by design. It must be attained with intentionality. One of the best ways to grow is to get around growing people. In fact, your life will generally be the same in ten years except for the people you meet, the books you read, and the experiences you have.

I'm glad you are reading this book, because it can shift your mindset and allow you to be mentored by a man who has learned transformative lessons from this journey, we call life. Alan Greenspan reminds us that "Experience is not what happens to a man; it is what a man does with what happens to him." My friend, George Amos, has taken what happened to him and, by God's grace, made a better man and a better life!

Many people ask the question, "If you could go back in time and give a message of advice to your younger self, what would you say to him/her?" But here is a better question that I want to challenge you to ponder: "If you could go ten or twenty years into the future, what would you hope to have become?" You have no power to change your younger self, but you definitely determine who and what you become in the future.

All change begins with a decision. Fear is a reaction; courage is a decision. You have to decide to take action and be different. Something has to **SHIFT** in your thinking, your mindset. The word "**shift**" comes from an Old English word that means to "**arrange, place, or order.**" In order to shift from where you are into something greater or better, you have to rearrange some things in your life. You have to rearrange your priorities. You have to place new focuses in your life. You have to reorder your daily disciplines.

Our modern word "**shift**" also comes from an Old Frisian word that means to **"decide, determine, or test."** As you prepare your life for *The Amos Shift*, you will be challenged to make some decisions, determine new courses, and test new strategies. If something does not challenge you, it will not change you. Embrace the challenge. Welcome new ideas. Allow yourself to be stretched.

I want you to think of your life like an automobile. In order for it to go faster, you have to shift gears. Driving uphill, you need to be in first gear; but you can't go very fast in first gear. When you get to the top of the hill, you'll need to shift into third, fourth or fifth gear. This enables the engine to travel faster with greater ease. As you age, you need to be able to travel faster with greater ease. That's what *The Amos Shift* will do for you. So, open your heart and mind, buckle your seat belt, and get ready to shift gears and be thrust forward!

SHIFT YOUR MINDSET

When you're not sure what the outcome will be
Shift Your Mindset
When the numbers associated with your life
are not adding up or coming out
Shift Your Mindset
When people, especially your loved ones, let you down
Shift Your Mindset
When you let yourself and others down
Shift Your Mindset
When you think you're down and out
Shift Your Mindset
When you need an answer to a pressing situation
Shift Your Mindset
When you've given your all and it's still not enough
Shift Your Mindset
When you receive a call that's not good news
Shift Your Mindset
When you have done things that you're not proud of
Shift Your Mindset
When you feel lost, lonely or need to level up your life
Shift Your Mindset
When you think your situation is impossible
Shift Your Mindset and say:
With God all things are possible

INTRODUCTION

THE AMOS SHIFT

Whatever you're going through. Whatever has come over you. Whatever you need to overcome to live the life you imagine – know that as you shift your mindset, your life will shift for the better. All that you could hope for or imagine, plus more, will be your life's portion.

Things might not be exactly the way you want them to be. but if you're reading this book – they will get better. Regardless of your present situation, God has a plan and purpose for your life. Even if it doesn't seem that way now. When you make the decision to be, do, and have more and put God first, it will be so.

When I was a teenager, a car with a manual transmission, or manual shift, was what we called a "stick." Most of my friends knew how to drive that type of car. A stick, back then, normally had 5 gears- as pictured- this was the shift pattern. I show this picture, because some young folks today have probably never seen what a stick looks like.

Me and my brothers learned to drive a stick by watching my Dad and uncle. That was the only type car my family owned. We had to learn how to drive it or catch the bus. We could determine what gear the car needed to be in based on our speed.

Or we could listen to the sound of the engine to change gears. When the engine "revved" up, we knew it was time to change gears. To change gears, you had to use your left foot to press in the clutch, take your right foot off the gas, use the stick to shift gears, then ease off the clutch and accelerate, all at the same time. To begin motion, the car had to be in 1st gear to move forward. After each 20-mile increase in speed, it was time to shift gears. Driving a manual transmission car involves a simple series of motions that, once learned, become automatic.

Often times in life, we get stuck by not listening to the still, small voice within telling us it's time to shift. The voice is saying, "Shift, you've been in first gear for way too long." We, on the other hand, continue to drive on the interstate in 1st gear.

If you never shift, eventually you will ruin the transmission. Or even worse, blow the motor because it was time for a shift and you decided to drive on the interstate going 70 miles per hour in 1st, 2nd, 3rd or 4th gear when you should have shifted to 5th gear. The car will run in a lower gear, but it will not run at full capacity.

Likewise, you can survive operating in a lower gear but, like a car, it will not be at full capacity. Why settle for 1st gear when God is trying to get you in overdrive. Because we are creatures of comfort, we'll settle for driving on the interstate in 1st gear and eventually blowing the motor. All because we wouldn't listen to that still, small voice that says, "Go, you can do it, shift go to the next gear, I got you."

I remember when I left Illinois to move to Atlanta without a car. I was catching the bus and driving my sister's friend's car. My vehicle was back in Illinois being worked on. After a few months in Atlanta, I went back home to get my car.

I caught a Greyhound Bus from Atlanta back home because of limited funds. The bus ride was a 15-hour journey. I was beyond fed up with this bus stopping every hour to pick up more passengers. I told myself that after I got off this bus, I will never get on another bus again.

I arrived in Illinois the next day and went to my mechanic to pick up the car and head back to Atlanta. I was happy as a pig eating slop! I got myself some wheels!

When I got about an hour into the drive, the car temperature gauge started to run up too hot. I'm like, "Oh my, this is the same problem I was having when I left the car." I left the car because I needed head gaskets. My shade tree mechanic told me my car was fine and he had fixed the problem.

About 30 minutes up the road, all hell broke loose. White smoke was everywhere. I knew immediately what the problem was because I'm somewhat mechanically inclined. My 1984 White Buick Park Avenue was dead!

I was on limited funds with enough money to get enough gas for two tanks which would've put me in Atlanta. Fortunately, I made it to a gas station and called my Dad to tell him, "Pops looks like I'm stuck, I got to be at work Monday morning, I have a few dollars in the middle of nowhere in Lebanon Indiana."

By this time, I was worrying about what to do. Dad calls me back on the pay phone at the gas station and says, "Well flights are too high, so that's out, we are coming to get you and take you to Atlanta."

I didn't know how to take his response at the time. My first thought was, Dad is thinking, "Oh no! This boy has caused so much trouble. He is not coming back here." Then my second thought was, just maybe he wants me to stay on this path. "That's my boy and he is on to something."

My Dad and Uncle Russel picked me up in Indiana and drove me to Atlanta. They then turned around and drove right back Illinois. My Dad went back the next day, picked the car up and took it home.

Now, I realize that was a shift. I was trying to do something and God was trying to shift me into another gear. I was trying to choose reverse and the Master had another plan. I told you that I was on limited funds. Right? The vehicle was not paid for. It had already been behind four payments and the bank was looking for it. God was saying to me, "Son you are not going to take that extra baggage into your new life. I'm shifting you from your old way of thinking to a new way. Leave the baggage behind."

The car breaking down required me to leave it. If I had brought it to Atlanta with me, it would have been more problems. The "Repo Man" came and got it and that was the end of that. Sometimes we don't see the blessing because of the circumstance. When God shifts your circumstances and situations, it is life changing and ends up being epic.

I am George Amos, Jr., the CEO of Computer Cabling of GA, Inc., a megachurch marriage ministry leader, minister to men - with my own clothing and accessory line. I am a product of grace and that is why I have decided to share my experiences with you, to give you a deeper insight and understanding of the power of God's grace. His grace, took me from being labeled a felon, to traveling first-class, all over the world, feasting on the best cuisines. I have been places that I did not know existed and stayed in hotels fit for a king. God's grace allowed me to do all of this, plus more, without having a formal education.

I give God the credit for my success. I share my accomplishments and story with you, not to brag or boast, but to encourage you to put aside your fear and level up your life with faith. God has done wonderful things for me and He desires to do great things for you too. The bottom-line is, If He did it for me, He will do it for you- providing you do your part.

I wrote this book to help you shift your mindset to level up your life to live a more significant life. It is packed with powerful principles to help you live with more purpose, power and most of all love. You will find thought provoking questions and exercises at the end of each chapter to help you benefit from your reading. My hope is that by sharing stories from my life you will be inspired. I give you an opportunity to capture thoughts pertaining to your life, you will be inspired to trust God and believe that He has great plans for you too, despite what you are currently going through.

If you are striving for purpose or a better life, but there seems to be nothing pushing you forward, this book is for you. *The Amos Shift* will help you shift your mindset, level up your life to embrace a life that welcomes God's grace upon you to be prosperous and make a difference in the lives of others.

As you turn the proceeding pages, please take the time to reflect upon your past, look within to make sense of your present, and always look to God to embrace the phenomenal future He has in store for you.

> Can two walk together, unless they are agreed?
> AMOS 3:3 (NKJV)

SHIFT 1

TAP INTO THE ROOTS OF YOUR LIFE

How often have you asked yourself these questions: What makes me who I am? What is my purpose? What am I supposed to do with my life? I pondered those questions for many years. As I mulled the questions over, I realized that my past experiences played a key role in making me the man I am today. The thoughts I had when making decisions in my life were affected by my life's experiences. The cumulative effect of our roots, both good and bad, is the way we make sense of our reality.

> "If you know where you are from, it will be harder for people to stop you where you are going."
> — MATSHONA DHLIWAYO

For this purpose, let's agree that your roots refer to the principles inherent in your background, the values you hold strongly and the core spirituality you possess that makes you who you are. Your roots refer to the factors that molded and shaped you into who you are now. Tapping into your roots means freeing yourself from the traumatic memories and experiences of your past. That is, letting go of the fear holding you down and finding your purpose in God.

I am one of nine siblings, five boys and four girls. Sometimes I laugh when I think of all the hard work my parents, George and Trollie, put into not only making, but providing for nine babies. Now that's something that's definitely a rarity today. I have great memories of growing up. The highlight of that time is playing the games Monopoly and Trouble and eating peppermint candy every Christmas. Year after year, we did the same thing. My siblings and I always looked forward to receiving our gifts. My Mom would manage to save a little money throughout the year to make sure we had a little something under the Christmas tree. More than likely, it was something we needed like socks, underwear or something to wear. If we were lucky, we would get a little toy every now and then.

On a few occasions when we did not get anything on Christmas, we knew we would just have to hope and wait until the beginning of the New Year when my Dad was paid.

With a family of 11, finances were challenging. We did not have much when it came to money. As they say, money was funny. Somehow, someway, our parents made a way. In the summers, we would press on with our homemade bicycles and makeshift toys. When I think of that time in my life, everything felt so good to me. We had no idea that money was funny until we were in our teens. As such, we lived a simple and fun life as kids. Reflecting upon that time, I often wish that I had cherished that time of my life more. That was a time in my life when I felt truly at peace without a care in the world.

My parents were born in Mississippi. Like many other African American families during that time, they migrated to Chicago in search of better opportunities. Every year we visited my relatives in Mississippi. I still remember going there every summer. All 11 of us piled in one car. Back then, seat belts were non-existent and our folks piled us in. My Dad never got a van or station wagon, because he was a cool cat and a van would have cramped his style. In looking back, I guess he felt, upon his return home, he could not be or look cool in a van. Let the truth be told, we probably needed a small bus.

It was a nine-hour drive to Mississippi, one way. The ride was uncomfortable for us. Dad on the other hand did not feel any of the discomfort because he had plenty of room. We were packed in that Chrysler 300 like sardines. Some kids in the back window, some in the front seat with Mom and Dad. Back in 1971, vehicles were made with that long front seat that was as long as the back seat. During the trip, we would try to get trucks to blow their horns. We would play the first person to spot the police wins' game too. Of course, that was encouraged by Dad since he was well over the speed limit. After we were tired of that game, we would say to one another "don't touch me" repeatedly. Can you believe it, eleven people in the car and we had the nerve to say don't touch me?

Those were really the good old days growing up with my brothers and sisters. We had fun and everything felt good. We were oblivious to what we had or did not have. Because both my parents worked, we all had to chip in to do chores. One thing for sure, work never ended as long as my mother, whom we affectionately call Trollie, was around.

My grandparents, who lived a few miles up the road, had a garden. There were periods in our life that our day started at 5 a.m., as we were all responsible for doing our part to plant and water peas, beans, and other vegetables. Trollie started us working at a very young age. I still remember those five a.m. wake up calls. To this day, I am an early riser.

Trollie would turn on the lights in our room and say, "get-up, it's time to go." Trust me, you already knew staying in the bed was never an option. It was not a democracy but a dictatorship, and Trollie was the boss of us all.

We would get dressed, grab buckets, shovels, hoes, load the car and get to it. The farm was about ten minutes from our home. It consisted of two acres of farmland, where the real work went down: digging, shoveling, hoeing, plowing and planting. Trollie had such a strong work ethic. She was incredible and drilled the values of hard work, religion, and respect for others into us at an early age. Her strong work ethic influenced me strongly and played a vital role in pushing me to where I am today.

While growing up, Trollie demanded that we get along with each other, be honest and above all, show respect to adults and others. My parents were into the teaching, do as I say, not as I do. I realize now that more is caught than taught -what we do or don't do, speaks louder than the words we speak.

As a kid, I just didn't understand why we needed to get the belt put on our behinds so often. Nevertheless, I said I grew up in a dictatorship, not a democracy. Talking and reasoning with our parents was not part of the equation. If we did something wrong, you best believe a whipping was coming. Trollie used to say, "It hurts me more than it hurts you to have to beat you, but if I spare the rod, I'll spoil the child."

In some ways, I believe all those whippings made me and some of my siblings rebellious. At the end of the day, doing it right, being right and working diligently to pay our way, was reinforced so much that when we did go astray – we never drifted too far from the Amos family core values.

As I got older, hustlers, not farmers appealed to me. The stylish clothes they wore, the shiny cars they drove, the pretty women surrounding them and the big money wads that they flashed caught my attention. In my community or "hood" as it was referred to, the hustlers were always clean, didn't have dirt under their nails and seemed to be having all the fun. Around that time, I became more attuned to my family's needs and the lack of funds. There was also desire within me to be recognized, affirmed and accepted by the "cool people" in the community.

I'm not happy to admit it, but this was a point in my life when I seriously considered selling drugs. My best friend, who I consider a guiding star in my life, talked me out of it. Instead I ended up hustling "hot goods". If you're not from the "hood", "hot goods" are items that are acquired the non-conventional way. These items are not purchased but they are acquired in another manner. Simply put, they are stolen.

When you grow up with eight other siblings – you learn how to get along with others. You learn how to treat others and you learn how to get others to do things for you. I learned from my family how to be a good hustler. The people in my community loved to see me coming with the goods at a great price. Not only did I bring them something that they wanted at a great price – but I also made them feel good about purchasing it from me.

This went on for a while. There was money in my pockets and women chasing me. I had the stuff I wanted: a car, clothes and cash – just like what the ones I looked up to in my hood had. Nobody could tell me anything, not even my dear Trollie, who tried to warn me that I was on the wrong track.

If you don't glean anything else from this book, always remember that the most important thing a person will ever tell you comes after they say "but." But, that period in my life was short lived. I ended up getting arrested and stayed in jail for 90 days, because bail was not an option. That was the lowest period in my life. The time spent in the slammer changed me forever. Afterwards, society labeled me a felon which impacted how I lived my life. I was unable to get certain jobs. After being released, the construction industry is where I was able to become gainfully employed. It's hard for me to put into words, how happy I was to put on a pair of carpenter's pants and get my hands dirty. So much for being flashy for a while.

Reflecting upon my past, leads me to acknowledge the fact that the grace of God was always at work in my life. The challenges I went through after being labeled a felon could have held me back. Because of God's grace, I was eventually able to have my record expunged with a pardon from the governor. Even when I veered away from my core values, God was still present. He used and still uses, everything that I went through to bring Him glory.

God's plans for my future were bigger than the pain and regrets of my past. With His grace, I was able to pull myself up and move forward. What I am saying is that your experiences can either make or mar you depending on what you want and what you choose to believe for your life. Your past should be your stepping-stone and not your hindering block. Stop judging yourself because of the mistakes that you have made. If God doesn't judge or hold what you have done in the past against you, then why should you?

When we accept the labels society places on us, we take God out of the equation. You will always have a choice with God. You can decide to believe or not to believe in Him. He will never force Himself upon you. Once you decide to believe in Him. He will make things right in your life. He will make things better than you can imagine at this moment of your existence.

I know it might be hard for you to believe in someone you can't see. While you can't see Him- when you begin to live your life with Him – you will feel Him. His love will flood your heart and people who follow Him will appear in your life who are sent from Him to bring solutions, lessons and love.

Although He is an invisible God, I am a living witness that He can and will do what seems to man impossible or hopeless. He will make the crooked things in your life straight, just like He did for me. If you need proof – it's in the Bible.

> "In all your ways acknowledge Him, And He shall direct your path."
> PROVERBS 3:6 (NKJV)

Mind*Shift* **#1: Tap into The Roots of Your Life**

What needs to be straightened out in your life?
_____

**I decree that from this day forward, I choose to shift my mindset to level up my life. I live my life with hope, faith and belief in God.
I choose to believe that nothing is impossible.
I know that God's grace is given to me freely and I will suddenly see the manifestation of that which I need, hope for and desire.
In Jesus' name, Amen!**

SHIFT 2

STUDY YOUR NAME

It is said that, "it is not what we're called but what we answer to that matters." I was named after my father. I'm a junior. Although I was named after him, I never answered to the fact that I was a "mini-him." I always felt like my own man with a drive to be my own person.

> "Names have power."
> RICK RIORDAN

I'm reminded of George Foreman, who named of his five sons George. There's a George Foreman Jr, George Foreman II, George Foreman III, George Foreman IV, and George Foreman V. Now, that is in keeping with the belief that the highest honor a man can give his son is his name. I guess that's why I was named after my Dad and chose to name my son after me. Knowing that there's someone whose name is George Amos III, has been like a wind behind my back, pushing me to live in a manner that makes him look up to me favorably.

In the past, a person's name meant something. During my Dad's days – people were named after characters in the Bible.

Nobody ever told me the meaning of my name. All I knew, was that I was named after my Dad. I think I did hear at one point that the name Amos was in the Bible. But I never took the time to open the book and read what it said. After researching my first name, I discovered that the name George meant tiller of the soil or farmer, which led me to reflect upon my days as a little boy.

Deep down inside, I really enjoyed it when we used to work on my grandmother's farm from sun up to sun down. Even though it was hard work, as Trollie cracked the whip, there was something about the dirt that made me feel grounded and connected with something bigger than myself. The fresh air and nature always cleared my head and calmed my soul. When the crops grew, an enormous sense of pride welled up within me. To know that I planted the seeds that resulted in food for us to eat was truly amazing.

Society has gotten away from using names of past generations. If your first name is uncommon, ask your parents to tell you the meaning or origin of your name. Clues about who you are can also be revealed in your last name. I gained so much revelation about myself when I finally took the time to read the book in the Bible titled Amos. Studying about Amos provided me with more clarity about my life, while validating the future call on my life. Amos was a sheepherder and sycamore fig farmer. He farmed to supplement his income from herding sheep. In today's world he would have been considered an entrepreneur, like me.

In the Bible, God used people to deliver messages to His people. His Spirit would come upon the people He selected and they would speak messages that He gave them. Sometimes He used them to warn the people of devastating weather situations. Sometimes they spoke words of correction to the people when they went against His commandments. Sometimes they spoke words of direction by providing insight from God concerning the future or wisdom to deal with a situation.

The term referred to people He used in that manner was Prophet. The books, in the beginning of the Bible, are named after prophets, because they wrote the books while playing a pivotal role in the history of Christianity. There were even Schools of the Prophet, for people called by God to learn how to hear His voice and deliver His message.

Amos did not start out as a prophet and he did not go to a School of the Prophet. He was focused on his business of herding sheep and farming figs, but God still used him, because he had compassion for the people. God used Amos to hold His people accountable for their ill-treatment of others. Amos spoke words that pointed out the failure of the people to fully embrace God's idea of justice.

Because, during Amos' time on earth, the rulers in his city were selling off needy people for goods. They took advantage of the helpless and oppressed the poor. The men used the women immorally. Many of the "elite" people were drunk on their own economic success and intent on strengthening their financial position. The people had lost the concept of caring for one another. God used Amos to rebuke them, because He saw in their lifestyle evidence that they had forgotten God's commandments.

God's word, through Amos, was directed against the privileged people who had no love for their neighbor, who took advantage of others, and who only looked out for their own concerns.

Amos was a person of significance. He cared about making a difference in the lives of others. He could have lived his life in a comfortable manner and we would not know who he was today. Although I have been serving in ministry for a couple of decades, I feel a burden to do more. While researching my name, I discovered a clue as to why. Low and behold, I discovered that the name Amos means burden or burden bearer.

I think by now, that you're getting the message of just how important our names are. Our names are who we are, the mark of our identity. If you are like most people, you love your name and get angry when someone mispronounces or misspells it, but how can you feel that way without even knowing what your name means? By understanding its meaning, you can start to better understand who you are. You might notice some similarities between it and your characteristics, as I did.

Once you embrace the value of your name, you'll have a greater insight into your identity. I can confidently say that most, if not all, names have significance. After researching my name, I take pride in having such a strong name. I wished I had known sooner what it meant. Although my parents said they just named me after my father, it amazes me to learn just how much of the meaning of my name that I embody.

I named this book *The Amos Shift*, not just because my last name is Amos, it has a far deeper meaning. The Prophet Amos was used by God to describe the consequences that would come on the people who had turned their backs on Him by failing to follow His commandments. When the people did wrong or sinned against God's commandments, they would have to make a sacrifice by taking one of their animals to the priest to slay on the altar for their sins. As you read the Bible more, you'll discover that God did amazing things for the people, but time and time again, they did things against His will, laws and commandments.

No matter what the people did, God still loved them. It is our children that teach us the true meaning of unconditional love. We provide for our children, even when they can't give us something in return. We love them even when they are disrespectful or go astray. God sees us as His children and loves us even more than we could imagine. He loved us so much so that He made a way for us to be forgiven for the things we do that are not aligned with His words, will, ways, and teaching. The very first scripture I had to learn was John 3:16.

> For God so loved the world that He gave His only begotten Son, that whoever believes in Him should not perish but have everlasting life.
>
> JOHN 3:16 (NKJV)

What that scripture means is God's son, Jesus, now serves as our sacrifice when we have sinned. Because Jesus was born of a virgin, lived a sinless life, died on the cross and ascended into heaven in three days, God no longer requires that animals be sacrificed on the altar. The blood that Jesus shed on the cross over two thousand years ago serves as our sacrifice. So, when we need God to do something for us, we must first repent for what we have done. Then ask to be forgiven in the name of His son Jesus.

I would never tell you what to do or stop doing. God guides us through His word in the Bible. He gives us a choice to follow Him or not. I can say without a shadow of a doubt, you will always end up on top when you decide to follow His guide.

The Amos Shift is a judgment free zone. We all have something going on that we could be judged for. The Amos Shift is about calling you up to who you are, because of God's love for you. In the spirit of my namesake, I have a burden to see you set free of the limits you place on your life. I have a burden to share with you my story, with the hopes of it inspiring you to dream bigger, live richer and leave a mark in the earth that cannot be erased, because after all, God knows your name.

> And I will make you a great nation. I will bring good to you. I will make your name great, so you will be honored.
>
> GENESIS 12:2 (NLV)

MindShift #2: Study Your Name

When people say your name or think of you, what do want them to think or say?

I decree that my name will bring honor to God.
When others think of me,
they will have good thoughts.
They will remember the fact that I made them feel good.
They will be inspired by me to reach higher,
dream bigger and live with integrity.
In Jesus name, Amen!

SHIFT 3

LOOK WITHIN TO LEAD

The more I understand who I am, the more effective I am in life. As I come to grips with what drives me and who God made me to be, the more I am driven to be and become all that He intended for me to be. In my early years, I thought life was all about having and getting.

> "Your vision will become clear only when you can look into your own heart. Who looks outside, dreams; who looks inside awakes."
> — CARL JUNG

I thought I had to make more money to get more things. The more I got, the more I wanted; and I was never satisfied. In search of more happiness and satisfaction, I found myself making a list of my strengths, weakness, opportunities and threats. In business, that list is referred to as a SWOT Analysis. My SWOT Analysis enabled me to work towards becoming a better person. It has helped me embrace my leadership abilities, staff my weaknesses and lead my life in a manner that honors my maker.

If you are reading this book, then you are a leader too. The way you lead your life will determine the life you lead. When things aren't going so well, it's easy to think the problem is "because of them." When things aren't going right for us, the problem is never "because of them" and the problem is never another person. You might not believe me but, I'm telling the truth.

If there's a pattern that keeps showing up in your life – it's on you. For instance, if each month you have to borrow money to pay your rent, is it someone else's fault that you failed to manage your money? Alternatively, is it someone else's fault, that you chose not to prepare yourself for a job that pays more?

If you keep blaming your parents, spouse, "the man" or keep saying, "It's all about you not being able to get a break", yet you refuse to do something about the situation, that's a problem on the inside, not the outside.

Stephen Covey, Ph.D. said, "Anytime we think the problem is "out there," that thought is the problem." Yet, the truth is, the times we need to hear what Covey or any other thought leaders say on the subject is often when we resist it. It takes a strong foundation of self-confidence, self-acceptance and self-worth to look inside, but it is one of the best things you can do for yourself.

> "Watch your thoughts, they become words; watch your words, they become actions; watch your actions, they become habits; watch your habits, they become character; watch your character, for it becomes your destiny."
> — UNKNOWN

Taking the time to look within yourself, will enable you to lead a more meaningful life. Before you can lead anyone, you must lead yourself. Every aspect of your life is impacted by leadership. Your current situation is a result of how you decided to lead your life.

Many years ago, I stumbled upon a piece that has provided great guidance to me.

To this day I am very careful about what I say. If it's not positive, then I don't say it. Back in elementary school we learn, "if you don't have anything nice to say, then don't say it." There have been many times, I've heard someone say, "he ain't gonna be nothing – he's just like his daddy." Can you imagine growing up hearing these words spoken over you as a child: "you will never amount to nothing;" "you won't be anything!" It is inevitable that after a while, the young person hearing those words begins to assume actions and habits that dictate behavior associated with losers.

On the other hand, when words of affirmation or encouragement are spoken over an individual's life, those words become a part of their psyche. Growing up hearing, "You are talented; You are great at helping people; You are an excellent problem solver; You have a knack for making people laugh; You will do phenomenal things with your life," will no doubt provide inspiration to help that person develop a character to sustain a great destiny.

It does not matter whether or not you heard words of affirmation growing up. What matters is how you elect to lead your life from this day forward. Regardless of your situation, there is always something you can do to improve yourself and your situation.

If you ever reach a point in life when you stop growing or improving – you might as well stop living. It is God's desire for you to prosper in all areas of your life. And to do so, you must make a choice to change the way you look at your situation. Speaking words that speak to your future will help you develop the habits to see those things manifest in your life. Should you want to go a little deeper and see even greater results, try googling what God says about you and your life. Afterwards, speak those words back to Him by thanking Him for what He said. You have power to access, through your phone, every single one of the promises God has in store for you. If you elect to follow through – I know you will discover that He has plans for your future, plans to prosper you, plans to give you the victory in your life, situations and more.

What type of life do you really want to lead? Many, many years ago, I decided to own my own home with no mortgage or monthly car notes. At the time I made that decision, I was living in an apartment with no idea how it would happen. I was living from paycheck to paycheck, with not enough check to meet my monthly obligations. But deep within me, I knew that all things were possible with God on my side.

Once I spoke those words, I began to take God at His word by believing His promises. I started to put aside people, places and things that did not align with the vision in my heart for my life. Suddenly, I no longer had a taste for alcoholic beverages or clubbing. I didn't even realize the impact that satisfying those desires had on my life. I was not aware of how doing those things became habits that were guiding my life. The time and money I spent hanging out and indulging in alcoholic beverages delayed me from preparing myself to pursue the destiny that God had in store for me.

There is a saying, "if you always do what you've always done, you will always get what you always got." In other words, if you want something different or if you want your life to be different, you must do something different. When I started to do different things – different people and different things began to appear in my life.

The friends who I hung out with had a hard time relating to me without me doing the things we used to do together. Since I was not hanging out anymore, I had more time to spend alone. During my alone time, I was able to look within to discover things about myself that I never knew existed. I realized that I had a gift of gab, an ability to see things to completion and plenty of charisma, just to name a few of my strengths.

On the other hand, I became acutely aware of my shortcomings or weaknesses, as SWOT Analysis revealed. I realized that if I wanted to earn more money – I needed to enhance my skills. Taking advantage of the opportunity to make myself more marketable, enabled me to ward off certain threats upon my life. The training acquired during that time prepared me to be gainfully employed, while equipping me to flourish in the technology industry. Had I not gotten the training back then -- I would not be doing what I'm doing today or generating the income that I do.

This was the time in my life when I started going to church more frequently. I began to connect with new people who were not perfect, but striving to be better. I have been asked many times, is it necessary to go to church? My answer is that the church is really a hospital for people who need spiritual and sometimes physical healing. Once the healing occurs, then it becomes a place to go to be equipped to help others lead more productive lives.

Church is a place where you go to learn about the ways of God. A good pastor will help you to understand the Bible and how to apply it in your everyday living. I was blessed to end up at a church where the pastor is an excellent teacher who inspired me to want to study the Bible on my own. By studying the Bible and applying Biblical principles in my life, amazing things began to happen for me. The opportunity to purchase my business happened during this time. I became a leader over a ministry at my church. I made amends with my oldest daughter. I was able to help family and I made more money than I ever dreamed possible.

I've worked very hard for all that I have, including the meaningful relationships I have with others. Through it all, I have a peace within that makes the hard work bearable. One Biblical principle that I adopted and practice to this day is tithing. Tithing is merely giving the church 10 percent of your earnings. It does not matter how much you earn; God just wants you to be faithful with the 10 percent. In the Bible, the book of Malachi 3:10, refers to this principle. It also states that when you are faithful with your tithes, God will bless you exponentially.

Please know that God does not need your money. He will bless you whether or not you tithe. But I am a living witness that when you do, He will make sure that more of whatever you give, comes back to you. Being obedient with my tithes over the years has definitely had a bearing on, not just my business success, but every aspect of my life.

McDonald's Big Mac consist of two all-beef patties, special sauce, lettuce, cheese, pickles, onions on a sesame seed bun. The secret sauce of my life has been tithing. Because I know God's word is true, if you try it –it will end up being a secret sauce that will help lead the life you identified.

SWOT ANALYSIS

Take a moment to list your strengths, weaknesses, opportunities, and threats. Set a plan in motion to utilize your strengths, develop your weaknesses, seize your opportunities and combat your threats.

My Strengths	My Weaknesses

My Opportunities	My Threats

Mind*Shift* #3: Look Within to Lead

List three actions you will take to develop your weaknesses.

I decree that God made me to be a leader and to triumph
over all situations that come my way.
The plans He has for my life will enable me to prosper.
I believe the biggest room in the world
is the room for improvement.
Therefore, I will strive to be a better me each day I live.
In Jesus Name – Amen!

SHIFT 4

CELEBRATE YOUR GUIDING STAR

The plan God has for your life includes people to show you the way and light your path. In life, you will need people to open doors for you. You will need people to help you get done what needs to be done and people that He will use to release resources to you. I've heard these three people referred to as door openers, doers and donors.

> "We do not understand the intricate pattern of the stars in their courses, but we know that He who created them does, and that just as surely as He guides them, He is charting a safe course for us."
>
> BILLY GRAHAM

There have been many people in my life who lit the way for me. My mother, who has gone on to be with the Lord, was by far, my biggest fan. Her love for me continues to push me to my destiny. She was a strong woman who never made excuses. She loved us all with every fiber of her being. Her love for my Dad was a true example of unconditional love.

I was blessed to have an uncle who was a tremendous role model. He was a hardworking man who never let what he could not do stop him from doing what he could. While he did not have a college education, I truly believe he could run circles around anyone with one. He was a general contractor. I guess he figured – he would hire himself. I used to love working with him because he expected everyone to give it their all as he did the same right alongside you. He actually built his own home from the ground and purchased rental properties, too.

I had another uncle who lived in California. In my mind he was the coolest person that I had ever met. He drove a Jaguar back in the 70s and dressed to the nines. His profession was building golf courses. Little did he know, that, just his being left an indelible impression upon my life.

Many people touched my life in a profound way. In fact, everyone whom we have ever known develops us. I cannot help but acknowledge my childhood friend Barry. He helped me shift to do the right thing when the wrong thing was calling my name. He embodied what it meant to be a true friend. Whatever I did right, wrong or indifferent, Barry was there.

Back in the mid-80s, the crack cocaine epidemic was running rampant in urban communities. I had peers and family members whose lives were changed by trying it just one time. Crack was something new to my community. Crack cocaine, also known simply as crack or rock, is a free base form of cocaine that can be smoked. Crack offers a short but intense high. Users of the drug say it is the most addictive form of cocaine.

No one really knew what damage it was doing or the long-term effect it would have on the lives of people who used it or sold it. I witnessed some of the finest people in my neighborhood start looking like they were homeless. One thing was certain, many people were using it and many were buying it. I was definitely not a person who used drugs, but I was definitely a candidate to sell drugs.

As the crack epidemic grew, so did the money that people made from selling it. I saw young men go from just plain old broke guys standing on the corner with no job, no career and no promise -- to walking around with thousands of dollars in their pockets, riding around in the fastest cars and dating the prettiest women. That definitely caused me to take notice of these guys. I worked a couple of jobs, brought home little money after working my behind off every-day. Working 12-16 hours a day, making eight dollars an hour, gets old after seeing guys standing on the corner making thousands a day. I didn't make that much in a month.

In the back of my mind, I knew what they were doing was wrong and probably would not last forever. The idea crossed my mind to start selling crack to make big money and live a grander life. Morally I knew it was wrong, but from a financial standpoint, I couldn't help but give the idea serious consideration.

Eventually, I decided to talk to my buddy, Barry, about selling crack together. I told him that I thought we should do it and make us some of that fast money. Barry was scary. He was scared to do anything wrong. I was the one who was the risk-taker. I heard it said that, risk-takers are moneymakers. Be forewarned that not all risks are worth taking.

Although Barry may have had some thoughts about it, he said to me, "Nah Brooks, (which is my nickname) we can't do that, our parents taught us better than that." I said to Barry, "you're right, we can't do that. I'm out of here. I can no longer live the way we're living; I have to seek better for my life." Within the next year, I decided Atlanta was the place for me. I left both jobs I was working and moved to Atlanta. Barry, on the other hand, decided to stay in Illinois. One year later, I found out Barry had become one of the biggest drug dealers in the State of Illinois.

Several years went by and my relationship with Barry grew cold. We had not communicated with each other. Barry decided to visit Atlanta for Freaknik, which was an annual event that drew college students. He drove to Atlanta with some of his new friends. He had plenty of money. Not only was he driving one of his new cars, he had two other people driving two more of his cars.

We met at Lenox Mall. I was in disbelief at who Barry had become. He was definitely not the Barry I grew up with. The one I had called friend. At that point, my life had totally changed. I was no longer interested in hanging out, nor was I interested in hanging out with someone who was all-right with dealing drugs.

I met him, because I wanted to see with my own eyes who he had become. After a couple of hours, I told Barry I had to leave and told him to enjoy his time in Atlanta. Many years passed without me speaking to Barry. I thought of him often but was focused on making a life for my family and myself.

He called me a few years after our encounter and asked me if I could possibly keep a car in my yard. I declined and told Barry that was not something I could do. Not long after that conversation, Barry was arrested for selling drugs.

I found out Barry was looking at a 20-plus year sentence. Barry served 10 years and was recently released from prison. While he was in prison, I never took the opportunity to go see or talk to him until his final year of a 10-year sentence. During one of my recent visits home to see my family, I got the opportunity to see Barry. We met and talked. When we saw each other – it was heartwarming and yet tearful all at the same time.

I told him that I was sorry he spent 10 years in prison. I mentioned that I really owed him an apology. He asked me why did I feel I owed him an apology? I told him because his fate could have been mine had he not encouraged me not to sell drugs. I felt as though the time he spent in prison saved my life. If Barry had said, "Brooks let's sell drugs, I would have stayed in Joilet and more than likely spent years in the slammer.

I thanked Barry for being a true friend and for giving me the truth of who we were back in the day. Drugs wasn't then, nor is it now, a way to go. Barry assured me that it wasn't my fault. He said, "I chose the road I went down, you don't have to be sorry, I chose this road. I failed to shift forward my friend."

Today, I am grateful to have a friend that said no. Everybody needs a Barry. Everyone needs a friend who will say no when it is the right thing to do. As he picks up the pieces of his life, I am forever grateful to my friend Barry. It saddens me to say that he is on dialysis and has some form of a rhythmic heart issue.

Today, I take comfort in knowing I was able to reconnect with my friend. I keep him in my prayers and thank God that when it was time for me to shift forward – I did.

Another person who lit the way for me was Sha. I'm a firm believer that everyone needs a Sha in their lives. She is a family friend that is like a sister. We grew up together. We went to church together. She was friends with me and my sisters. She also dated my first cousin.

Sha moved to Atlanta approximately five years prior to me. Back in 1985, my cousin and I visited her in Atlanta and I absolutely fell in love with the city. At that time, I told her that Atlanta was the place for me and expressed a desire to move to Atlanta.

Fast-forward two years, Sha came home to Joliet for a visit, she called me up when she arrived and said to me: "Why don't you come on and move to Atlanta, you shouldn't be here in Illinois." I thought how can this be? How can I make it happen? It wasn't like I had a great career going, so I accepted and said okay, Sha I'm in!"

I moved to Atlanta with no money, no car, no job, and no education—nothing, but the call from Sha encouraging me to come to Atlanta! I now know that I heard a still, small voice within beckoning me to go. Little did I know, at the time, that decision would change the course of my life forever.

We left Illinois on a September morning. Sha picked me up and said, "Let's go…we're rolling out – Atlanta bound."

She lived in a one-bedroom apartment on Beecher Street, in Southwest Atlanta. I slept on her pull-out couch and the journey began. Sha was so kind and generous. She worked at night. I would drive her to work, drop her off, use her car and pick her up in the mornings. At the time, I was working a construction job.

She was going to school while working a full-time job and would often allow me to drive her car while she caught the bus to school. I'm still in awe of her actions, as I think about the sacrifices she made for a young dude with no plan. She believed in me when I didn't even believe in myself.

I am convinced that she acted on the call that God had on her life to propel me to my God-given destiny. I stayed with Sha for almost a year. She got so tired of me driving her car, she decided to purchase me a car on her credit card so I could get out of hers.

I had no idea, no real idea, of how much the sacrifices she made for me would bless my life. Sha literally gave up her life for a year so I could get on my feet. It really is possible for a friend to stick closer than your sister or brother.

Sha was sent by God to do what she did for me. Thirty years later I'm still in Atlanta, living my dream, thanks to a friend who believed in me when I couldn't believe in myself. She put action to her words. I owe this lady my life.

Everybody needs a Sha in his or her life. Sometimes we need to be a Sha for someone. We all need someone to believe in us, someone to help us through the rough patches of our lives. We need someone to dream for us when we can't dream for ourselves. Most of all, we need someone that's listening to God and prays for us when we can't even see our way! Without Sha, my life would have been totally different.

Whoever your Sha is, or whomever you are a Sha to, I pray that you will always celebrate the life that God chose for you to bless. I pray that you remember to call people up and not call them out. In so doing, you will have pleased the One who gave you the assignment and blessed you to be in a position to be a blessing.

Mind*Shift* #4: Celebrate Your Guiding Star

Who do you need to reconnect with to thank, celebrate or lift up in prayer? Or who will you commit to help without expecting anything in return?

_____

I decree that I am who I am
because of sacrifices made by others.
I show gratitude to those
who have helped me along the way.
I search my heart consistently and continually to make sure
I celebrate others without expecting anything in return.
In Jesus name, Amen!

SHIFT 5

LIVE REDEEMED

You have a choice in life. You can choose to let your circumstances define you or you can choose to live by God's definition. There are only three opinions that really matter in life: your opinion of yourself, your opinion of God and God's opinion of you. You do not have to do it now, but I encourage you to write down how you feel about yourself, what the Bible says about how God feels about you, and how you feel about God.

> "People, even more than things have to be restored, renewed, revived, reclaimed and redeemed; never throw out anyone."
> — AUDREY HEPBURN

It is not my intention to paint a picture of everything being always perfect in my life. I've mentioned that I spent 90 days in jail. I believe that had I not gone to jail, I probably would never have been able to re-discover myself and find myself in God. I would not have gotten the push that took me to where I am now. It took me time, but I realize that God is always ready to bless us, as long as we're ready to reach out to Him in faith.

As long as I live, I will never forget the day of my pardon. As the elevator stopped on the fourth floor in the courthouse, my thoughts were running wild as I prepared for what I hoped would be my final day of standing before a Judge. Questions bombarded my mind. What is the States Attorney going to say? Will he object to my petition to expunge? What is the Judge going to say? Will he object to my petition? As I waited for my name to be called, I tried to calm my mind.

I had already received letters from the state denying my petitions for expungement. During that moment, fear had placed a stranglehold on my thoughts and mind. I had been fighting this battle for five plus years, waiting for this moment. Fear had me shaking in my pants. Honestly, the Lord had spoken to me and confirmed that the battle was over, but I was still scared of not being pardoned.

To calm my nerves, I begin to ask myself: I thought your faith was much stronger than you are showing?

This is a question we all must ask ourselves: Is my faith what I say it is? Am I a believer or not? Do I trust Jesus Christ or not? You only find out who you really are when the heat is turned up. At that moment, I was sitting right smack dab in the heat of who I really was and who I was dependent on. Finally, I took a few deep breaths, which allowed my thoughts to calm down. Then I called on the One who is really in control of me and all situations or circumstances that come my way. After wasting twenty minutes worrying about the Judge and his response, I called on the One who is in control of the Judge. I prayed and

> For God hath not given us the spirit of fear; but of power, and of love, and of a sound mind.
> — 2 TIMOTHY 1:7 (KJV)

asked for peace and a calm spirit. This scripture came to mind and helped ground me during the moment.

Immediately, I shifted into overdrive as my faith in God gave me a calmness that I had never experienced before. I actually heard the voice of God say, "This Is Finished; the outcome is already in your favor." From that moment on, I had no worries, doubt or fear. Within 10 minutes, the State Attorney came back and asked, "Is there anyone here on the docket seeking expungement?" I said "yes." They called my name; I stood before the Judge, who asked the State Attorney were there any objections to this case of expungement? The State Attorney replied, "NO!" The judge said, "Nor do I." Then he hit his gavel and stated "case closed, petition granted!"

Finally! After years of living life with a mistake I made as a teenager, I felt freed from a mark on my record and reputation. As I walked out of the courtroom, I was free, on paper, from the mistakes I made in my past.

The memories of that day remain etched in my heart. I can remember the process like it was yesterday. The way God worked everything out, during that time in my life, made me want to know more about Him. While it did not happen immediately, the process taught me to never, ever, doubt what God says and to believe all things are possible.

After the hearing, I went downstairs to pay a fee to complete the paperwork of clearing my record. The clerk took my money and as she handed me my receipt, she said, "tell Mr. Amos, the Clerks' Office said congratulations, not many people get a second chance." My answer to her was, "I will tell him." The clerk did not realize that I was Mr. Amos. She thought that I was his attorney!

My life is a testimony to what is possible when you make Jesus the Lord of your life. I have been redeemed. It is because of my redemption that I have vowed to make a difference in the lives of other men. I am compelled to help others seize their dreams for a better life in their heart, hold onto their hopes and receive the same redemption that I have. The Bible says God is not a respecter of persons, what He has done for me, He will do for you.

If you have made mistakes or have a shattered past, I want you to know that, with God all things are possible. I want you to see your circumstance as a beginning for you to let God take control. It is only the beginning of something new. The beginning of becoming significant and making life better for others. I'm giving my life example to others so that they don't make the same mistakes I made. Let my life be an example of what to do and what not to do. I've been redeemed, so can you!

Over the years, the ways in which God has worked in my life has truly changed me from the inside out. I believe my life experiences, especially being pardoned, will be an example to other men. There is something deep within me to tell others that when you've made a mistake, admit it, then quit it.

Mind*Shift* #5: Live Redeemed

Who do I need to forgive to be set free?

I decree that there is not anything that I have done,
anything that I am doing or will do,
to make me not be accepted,
forgiven or loved by Christ.
Because I have been forgiven,
I choose to forgive others.
I no longer judge myself or anyone else.
I am redeemed, restored and live my life
free from negative thoughts
about my past actions and deeds.

SHIFT 6

NURTURE YOUR RELATIONSHIPS

There are people who will come into your life for a certain time period and then leave. Sometimes people will come for a certain reason and you might not know why, when they come. There are people who will come and stay for a lifetime. Those who stay for a lifetime, will more than likely be the ones who you both have agreed to treat each other with dignity and respect.

> "Relationships connect us to our destiny. They are like bridges. Wisdom is necessary to discern which to cross and which to burn."
> **Bishop Dale C. Bronner**

As we become wiser, we realize that it is possible to learn something from every one of our relationships, be them good or bad. I am a firm believer that we teach people how to treat us. If you are a type of person who doesn't like to be talked to negatively, and someone does just that, you can let the person know how feel. If they don't stop, you can remove yourself or ask them to leave if it is your property.

All of our relationships teach us about ourselves. The saying, "Birds of a feather flock together" Is so true. It's also true that they fly to the same place. If your friends are doing certain things that you do not do, sooner or later you will start doing it, they will stop doing, or you will get new friends.

When building solid relationships, it is so important to have someone who you can be accountable to. That person should be someone you look up to; you should respect how they live and treat others. Above all, they should have integrity and honor for God. Oftentimes, they are referred to as a mentor. For me, it is my pastor. Over almost two decades of knowing him, he continues to be someone who I look up to even though I don't spend much time with him. By the way, it is o.k. to have more than one mentor and you don't always have to know them to be inspired by them.

There is a man, Reginald Lewis, who was one of the richest African American men in the 1980s. He was the first African American to build a billion- dollar company. I read his book and was amazed and inspired that a Black man could do the things he did. In some small way, I looked up to him and looked within to discern that I was made for more.

You should also have peers, on your level, with high aspirations. They should be a good listener, an encourager, and not be afraid to speak the truth to you, even if it is not what you want to hear. You should be able to trust them and know that they have your best interest at heart.

Have people in your life who you can pour into. A good way to remember these three important relationships is to think of a cross. The higher point of the cross is your mentor, the one you look up to. The horizontal line on the cross are your peer relationships, they are your partners. They are the ones who are striving, like you, to be better in all areas and it is their desire to see you succeed.

I continue to be blessed to have good people in my life who help me along the way. I cherish all of my friends and thank God for them. As I grew as a person, different types of people entered my life. One of my friendships that I cherish is the one with my friend Terry Pendleton. He is a former major league baseball player.

Because of Terry's talents, he lives life on a totally different level from most of us. As I began to prosper in my business, it allowed me to meet new people and do more of things I like to do, which are travel, ride my Harley, help my family and leave a legacy in the hearts of others. Throughout our friendship, his insight and honesty have been valuable on so many levels in my life.

At the bottom of the cross are the people who you are mentoring. It doesn't matter how old or young you are. There will always be people you can learn from and help. Choose your friends wisely, for if you want to know more about a person find, out who their friends and associates are.

One of the greatest relationships you will ever have is the one with yourself. I am reminded of this parable shared with me a long time ago.

An old Cherokee teaches his grandson about life:

"A fight is going on inside me," he said to the boy. "It is a terrible fight and it is between two wolves. One is evil–he is anger, envy, sorrow, regret, greed, arrogance, self-pity, guilt, resentment, inferiority, lies, false pride, superiority, and ego."

He continued, "The other is good – he is joy, peace, love, hope, serenity, humility, kindness, benevolence, empathy, generosity, truth, compassion, and faith. The same fight is going on inside you–and inside every other person, too."

The grandson thought about it for a minute and then asked his grandfather: "Which wolf will win?"

The old Cherokee simply replied, "The one you feed."

The second important relationship you will have is with your mate. Your destiny can be found in the heart of your mate. If you find someone to hold your heart in their hand, without bringing harm – you've found not only a good thing, but a God thing!

The Bible says, when a man finds a wife, he finds a good thing. I found more than a good thing when I found my wife. Her name is Ruby. There's scripture that helps me remember just how blessed I am to have found my God thing.

> She is more precious than rubies; nothing you desire can compare with her.
> **Proverbs 3:15 (NIV)**

Her name is Ruby Yvonne. I call her Von and we have been married for 25 years. I remember our honeymoon as if it was today. We were at a resort in St. Thomas, US Virgin Islands having a conversation when a huge argument ensued. To this day, I could not tell you what it was about. I do remember walking out of the room fuming with anger. I walked down to the beach and had a conversation with me, myself and I.

I remember asking myself, "What in the heck have I done? I've married this woman… maybe way too fast. Oh, my God, I've made a mistake, is this what marriage is going to be like?"

Von and I married after dating less than a year. Within three months, we were living together and 6 months later we were married. She paid for the wedding, the rings, honeymoon, and even purchased our first home.

At the time, I was a struggling businessman with a dream. My wife never wavered on what she wanted and has stayed the course throughout all these years.

We lived or as some would say, "shacked up" in an apartment. After getting married, we moved to "her house". I recall sitting at the closing. The attorney said to me, "Sir, move back, you can't sit here, you are not a signer on the documents." At that moment, I felt less than a man. At the time I had bad credit, slow credit, no credit. I could not even pay attention. But my wife still chose to marry me.

I would not want my daughters to marry someone who was in my shape and would not recommend you do so either. The Bible says, first count the cost, then build. My wife said, "I'm going to pay the mortgage and you pay all the other bills."

All of this didn't sit well with me. I wanted her to wait until I got my credit together, then buy a house. I'm sure she said to herself, "Yeah right, wait on you to get your credit right then purchase a home? Nah big boy, if I do that, we will probably never get a home, waiting on you."

You see, she had her stuff together. She had a good job, good credit, good spending habits and knew how to budget. Although my heart was saying nooooo, don't do it, I agreed to begin looking for a home, as we sought to find a place that was suitable for both of us.

At the very beginning, I told her, "No deal if I have to listen to you tell me it's my house and if you don't abide by my rules, then you can get out of my house."

We pressed forward. She signed and we moved into "HER" our house. All was well for a while. Then a few years passed and money got funny. We begin to argue more and more. Von reminded me that it was her house and if I didn't like it, I could get out.

Her words cut me like a knife. After many arguments and tension in our marriage, I told her, "No problem, it's your house and I will leave." Divine intervention kicked in. We sought marriage counseling and she made an agreement not to ever remind me that it was her house again.

Fast forward a year or so and children came into the picture. The business started to boom. Von was a flight attendant and it was becoming more difficult to manage everything in her absence. Because the business was flourishing, I asked her if she was ready to quit.

She struggled with the decision to leave her job. Instead of outright quitting, she took a leave of absence for five years. Right at the five-year point, I asked Von to go get a cashier's check. I told her, "Pay off your house and keep it in your name since it's your house." She did and we both are just amazed at how the Lord has moved in our lives.

We ended up selling that home and built another one. We went from everything being in Von's name to everything in my name. I attribute our success to the Lord and being faithful tithers. We put 10% of our earnings in church through our ups and downs. We have never, nor will we ever, stop tithing and giving.

When you decide to be or become a faithful thither. I promise God will be faithful and honor His word.

I don't care what level of life you're on, or how much money you have, there will be times when you want to walk away from your marriage. You must put God first and be willing to follow God's divine order for the family.

There are thousands of books on relationships. What I know for a fact is, none of us are perfect. When we interact with others, it's important to remember that the only person we can change is ourselves. My wife is not perfect, nor am I. But we are perfect for each other and have made a commitment to honor our marriage vows and commitment to God.

As a leader of the marriage ministry at my church, I have counseled hundreds of couples. Throughout the years, I have concluded that when the man is committed to Christ, his wife is more likely to respect him. Secondly, I think if we take the time to listen to each other without having to prove a point, or be right, we'll work out the disagreements. Lastly, it's imperative that couples take time to spend quality time with each other consistently.

> Bring the whole tithe into the storehouse, that there may be food in my house. Test me in this," says the Lord Almighty, "and see if I will not throw open the floodgates of heaven and pour out so much blessing that there will not be room enough to store it.
>
> MALACHI 3:10 (NIV)

Mind*Shift* #6: Nurture Your Relationships

What will you do to show appreciation
to those who you care about?

I decree that I honor the relationships in my life
by treating others the way I want to be treated.
I seek to find out what others like
and give gifts that they like on special occasions
and for no reason at all.
I am blessed to bless and given to give,
without expect anything in return.
In Jesus name, Amen!

SHIFT 7

BE AND BECOME

For as long as I can remember, I loved clothes. With eight other sisters and brothers, dressing well was not a priority for my parents. They were focused on feeding us and making sure we had the basics. But like me, they were fond of clothes too. The saying, "apples don't fall far from the tree," is truer than true. And

> "Every man and woman is born into the world to do something unique and something distinctive and if he or she does not do it, it will never be done."
>
> DR. BENJAMIN E. MAYS

somehow, some way – they managed to scrape a few pennies together to buy them something special to wear. To this day, I remember times when my Dad came home with nice suits and ties and occasionally, my Mom would purchase herself hats and dresses.

One thing about growing up in the inner city- or the "hood", as we called it – you learn to be creative and express your individuality through your clothing. I've always had an eye for dressing for as long as I can remember

Because we are a product of our environment, my Mom wanted us to have nice things like our friends and started making our clothes. I vividly remember my junior high school graduation. I wanted a two-piece leisure suit, like the ones that everybody in my hood was wearing at the time. Lo and behold, my Mom hooked her boy up. She made me an original, polyester plaid suit, with blue checks and a white blazer. Boy, I hated that thing. But I made the best of it.

I made a few dollars cutting grass and went down to the local Klein's department store, up on Cass street, where everyone shopped, and picked me up some two and a half inch stacks or platform shoes. They were light brown on the top and tan on the sole. You could not tell me anything. I thought I was an Ebony Magazine Fashion Fair Model.

I am not sure why I don't believe anyone made fun of me. But from that day forward, I decided I would never wear hand-me-down or home-made clothes again. I decided that if someone was making my clothes – it would be a professional tailor of my choice.

It was during that period that I took to bootlegging clothes, which resulted in my felony. I thought clothes made the person. Don't get me wrong – people treat you based on your appearance. But who you are at the core of your being, communicates louder than the clothes you wear.

As I grew up and became a man, I started shopping at malls and boutiques. One thing about me is, I never wanted to see someone in the same thing I was wearing. I began to shop for my clothes and shoes at different places from where everyone else shopped.

Having the privilege to travel practically free has been a true blessing. During my trips, I have learned to pick up different things to wear in different countries. On my first trip to China, I had my first custom suit made. I entered the shop, picked my own fabric and told the tailor how I wanted the suit designed. He measured me and the next day I went to pick up my suit; for less than a suit at any discount store in the states. It had my name embroidered on the inside of the jacket.

When I put that suit on – you could not tell a brother nothing, not a thing! I loved how I felt in that suit and I reminisced back to the time when I made a declaration that I would have tailor made suits. Your words have power.

After the euphoric experience of having my suit made, I had some shirts tailored-made to fit me and my style. While my family went sightseeing, I was having a ball getting custom made clothes. I had to purchase more luggage to bring home the suits, shirts and coats that I had tailored-made in China.

With flight privileges, we travel as much as we can. After China, we planned a family trip to India. Unbeknownst to me, India was also known for making apparel. I got the unction to seek out someone to manufacture linen shirts, suits and slacks. I found someone to make all I wanted. Did I mention the prices? Did I mention the prices when I was in China? Let's put it this way, they were unbelievable. I fell in love with the prices and began to entertain the idea of designing my own clothing line.

Upon my return to Atlanta, I couldn't get out of my thoughts what I had experienced in China and India. Soon after, I decided to start a clothing line for businessmen. I asked myself how can I make this happen? I prayed about it and decided to go back to India and hopefully make the right connections to start my own clothing line.

Jag Wear Fashions was born. Why Jag Wear? Jag Wear is simply my initials in reverse. George Amos Jr., turned around is Jag. I decided to do classic styles, with a little extra attention to details, or sauce, on it. I was determined to offer a great price so everyone who wanted the clothing could experience a quality suit at a good price.

I had a few associates from India and asked each of them if they knew anyone who could help me with clothing, fabrics, etc. Back to India I went. While there, I received a couple of great contacts. I stayed at the Marriott Hotel in Mumbai. I had a driver who took me out every day to meet tailors and textile manufactures. Ironically, after sharing with him my reason for being there, he was interested in working with me.

Shortly thereafter my driver, Hasan and Yousef who are brothers and I, decide we would take on this daunting task of making and selling suits and linen. After visiting many manufacturers and tailors, we opened a store in India. The quest of making this dream a reality happened.

I traveled back and forth to India about four times a year. I opened a store there and began manufacturing clothes. We not only began making clothes, we manufactured, shoes, belts, shirts cuff links, etc. I was so excited about this venture. I employed Hasan and Yousef's family and became very good friends.

To see this dream come true has been a blessing on so many levels. It has allowed me to make a difference in the lives of others on another continent. The store is life changing for my partners because in India, you are either rich or poor. There is no middle class. We even purchased scooters for Yousef and Hasan to get around town.

I have become really close to this family who lives on the other side of the world. This venture fulfilled my dream and it fulfilled their dream of becoming part owners of a business. Only God can do such a thing. He is omnipresent working on my behalf in the United States and working on their behalf in India. He connected us to fulfill dreams.

I'm grateful and honored to have this experience. It baffles me sometimes to think, I have my own clothing line. Who would have thought that a boy from the projects in Illinois, who was arrested for stealing clothes, would design, manufacture and own his own clothing line, all while employing people thousands of miles away?

> **A man's heart plans his way, But the LORD directs his steps.**
> PROVERBS 16:9 (NKJV)

Mind*Shift* #7: Be and Become

What would you attempt to accomplish
if failure wasn't an option?

I decree that doors are opening for me
to do what God made me to do.
I will continue to trust Him
and know that His plans for my life
will unfold in due season.
In the meantime, I will seek to hone
in on the one thing I do best,
spend time perfecting it while serving others
with integrity and humility.
In Jesus name, Amen!

SHIFT 8

BE A SOLUTION

As I was establishing my roots in Atlanta in the nineties, I was hired to work in sales with a communication supply company. Getting that job was a blessing and definitely, a part of God's will for my life. On paper, I would not have been the most likely candidate. The company took a chance on me. I was then, and now, grateful.

> "A person who sees a problem is a human being; a person who finds a solution is visionary; and the person who goes out and does something about it is an entrepreneur."
> NAVEEN JAIN

It wasn't an easy job. It was a challenging task, but my gratitude, strong work ethic, and belief in God kept me going. I quickly skyrocketed and became the top salesman. Fortunately, I was able to get lots of training, which was instrumental to my development and success.

While working there, I met Bernard, a white guy from South Georgia. Only God could have connected us. Bernard called me Yankee. I called him Redneck. He was from South Georgia and drove a Ford F-150 with a gun rack in the back. In his leisure time he hunted and fished.

One day he suggested that we start a company. At the time, I was still employed at the communication supply company, in a comfortable position making a decent living, and didn't think twice about his offer.

Bernard was persistent and mentioned the idea of starting a business several times. Finally, I listened to his offer. He said, once again, "We would do good in business together, I'll install computers, and you sell products." I responded with, "Can I get back to you within a week?" I asked a close friend, Bobby, what his thoughts were. He said, "You mean quit your job, and go start business with someone you don't know. What about your Insurance, what about your steady income?" Bobby had several questions and doubts about why I should think about this move.

In my mind, I'm 29 years old. What's the worst thing that could happen? I'm single, with no money already. I can't drop under the poverty scale any further than I am. My mind was already made up. I'm going with this opportunity. This could be a once-in-a-lifetime opportunity. When Monday rolled around, my life would be changed forever. I once read a book by James Allen and I quote, "You are where you are based upon the choices you make, not the choices anyone else makes for you." So profound. This choice changed how I thought about life and even working for someone. I confirmed with Bernard, "Let's do this." One month later, we were moving into our own office in a North Atlanta suburb. Bernard installed wire and cable so we formed a team to sell and install. Bernard hired a few guys to take on installation jobs with him and I would drum up business from my contact list. I brought a few major customers with me. We were off and running.

Business started coming in; however, we were unable to keep up with the demand. Several manufacturers were not on board. After two years, business was strained and extremely tough. By this time, both sides of the business were hanging in the balance. Bernard could no longer pay my salary and I didn't have money to just hang around for something I was not vested in. When you are a renter, verses an owner, you tend to think differently about your options. An owner sees a faucet leak and repairs it. A tenant sees a faucet leak and calls the owner to repair or they just simply move to another property. There is not much responsibility in being a tenant and you have choices to leave or stay. The owner's choices are limited.

At that point, Bernard offered me my first opportunity for ownership into a sinking company. I would own 51% and he would own 49%, why? We heard there were opportunities for minorities' in government business. We spoke to our accountant, Marsha, got an attorney, and drew up the papers. Now, I'm an official owner of a sinking company.

I was so excited, but business didn't get better. It actually turned for the worse. Bernard could no longer deal with the pressures of bill collectors and slow business. He made me a proposition. He asked me if I was interested in taking over the business? At this stage of my life, things had really changed, I'm now more mature and have a greater understanding of business. The biggest thing was the God-factor functioning in my life. I had built a relationship with God and consulted with Him about all things concerning me. I knew what was going to happen next, because God told me so. When Bernard posed the question to take over the business, I was not at all surprised.

I took the offer to take over the business. He could leave and if business picked up, I would pay him. Marsha, our accountant, had spoken to me for a year, that one day I would drive a nice fancy car to drop off my taxes and accounting to her. We chuckled, but I believed this would happen. The papers were drawn up and Bernard and I parted ways.

From Employee to Owner! I took on all the debt and set him free. Bernard was ecstatic. By the way, so was I. I couldn't believe I owned my own company. I never took out a loan. I never went through formal schooling on how to run a business. The creditors' calling was nothing new to me, I'd experienced this before I ever started a business.

Within 6 months, the business did a major turnaround. Contracts began pouring in and I could no longer do it with just me and Nancy. I hired my brother, who was a college graduate. Nancy worked for me and was always supportive. There were some weeks I couldn't meet payroll and she stood by my side. I would always assure her that one day, money would not be our problem. Sure enough, business took off and contracts came in daily.

Wow, I made how much today? One hundred thousand dollars today. Someone, wake me up! Am I dreaming? Okay where is the hidden camera? Oh, wait! Incoming fax. Seriously? A contract for thirty- thousand dollars. Wow, another contract for forty- thousand dollars! Wait, incoming, another contract; thirty-thousand dollars. You mean to tell me, I just received three contracts totaling One Hundred Thousand Dollars? I've never so much as made sixty thousand dollars in one year. And today I make one hundred thousand dollars in one day! This can't be real. Shouldn't I have a college degree to get contracts for this amount of money? But I have a felony on my record! My credit report number was just above a high cholesterol number.

With all the odds stacked against me, My Lord would not allow me to be denied. Wow! I'm totally amazed at what's happening. I can only reflect on the day I began in business.

The company went from doing $150,000 per year to three million dollars per year. I am elated! At that point, I called all the creditors and settled my debt and business was booming. We hired more staff. I gained a full understanding that Bernard was set-up by God, to help move me into the place that God had for me.

In the beginning, my motives were to go into business, make a lot of money, and have houses and cars in at least three different states. However, my heart was changed to understand why I was in business: to be a resource for others. My main objective is to be a blessing to others and give others hope that if I can make it, they can too.

Within a relatively short time frame, I called my accountant to tell her that I was ready to pay Bernard for his portion of the business. She told me, "Do not pay him that much money." I told her I have no choice, I had to.

Bernard had no idea what the business was doing. I called him and scheduled a meeting. We met and I asked him, "Are you interested in receiving a check for dollars in the mid-to-high-five figures?" He said yes and we agreed on the dollar amount. Our respective attorneys drew up the paperwork and the deal was complete. I handed him a check. We shook hands and I told him after I gave him the check, "I hope to see you again."

It's been fifteen years without a word from Bernard. Marsha finally agreed, that I should have paid him the amount that I did. I told Marsha that Bernard needed to know that God is real in my life as-well as his. Through the highs and lows in business I've learned to never give up. I've been blessed beyond anything that I could have ever dreamed.

There are days that I've pulled over on the highway while riding my Harley because uncontrollable tears blurred my vision. I've literally pinched myself, after pulling over on the shoulder, thinking, "Is the life I'm living a dream or is it real?" What's happened to me can also happen for you, if you would only believe in God and yourself with all your heart, mind and being.

Mind*Shift* #8: Be a Solution

If you could solve any problem in the world,
what would it be?
_____

I decree that I am a problem solver
with a heart to please God by helping humanity.
I choose to do what is right and honor my word.
I believe God will help me
to flourish and prosper
and be an asset to my family
and community.
In Jesus Name, Amen

SHIFT 9

SEEK SIGNIFICANCE

When you get to a point in your life, when you have more years behind you than you do in front of you, the years in front of you become much more meaningful.

I spent many years of my life focused on surviving. As I began to make more money than I dreamed possible, I began to feel better about myself. I equated the amount of money I made with being successful. At the time, it was no greater feeling than to be able to actual pay off our house note, travel, purchase better cars, motorcycles and clothes.

> "What counts in life is not the mere fact that we have lived. It is what difference we have made to the lives of others that will determine the significance of the life we lead."
> NELSON MANDELA

As my business flourished, I was called upon by family time and time again. I was making money, but my bills were in proportion to what I was making. While I had extra cash to share, my family is big and there wasn't always enough to go around.

A dear friend told to do what I could without expecting anything in return. I took his advice and haven't regretted the times when I was able to help and when I was not.

There's always been something inside of me that made me want to do what is right even when I did wrong things. At age 20, I searched for affirmation in an environment where, having babies at an early age appeared to be normal and generational.

I began dating a young lady who decided she was going to remain a virgin until marriage. I thought, "Wow, that's great, she will remain faithful to me while I continue my quest to seek and conquer." She dated me faithfully for over a year. I made my rounds around town with other girls, while increasing the pressure on my girlfriend to give in to my sexual demands. After finally succumbing to the pressure of my full-court press, in November 1982, my oldest daughter was born out of wedlock. My girlfriend, a 17-year-old mother, was filled with hopes of a future with me, a 20-year-old boy with no plan or vision for the future.

I was uncommitted to the lordship of Jesus Christ. I spent five years running in place with no vision, no plan and a 5-year-old daughter who was growing daily. Change seemed impossible. My future wasn't bright, and I saw no light at the end of the tunnel. The possibility of my daughter having married parents was slim. Basically, my daughter's dreams were shattered. She was added to the casualties of my past, a past that covered me with a tremendous amount of guilt and anger.

Through it all, I knew life had something more to offer than the road I was traveling. When I moved to Georgia, I did not know that I could change the place, but the people and the self-serving behavior of the past would come along. Once I settled in Atlanta with a job and residence, I became a seasonal dad. I visited my daughter in Chicago during the summer breaks and occasionally on the weekends. I bought my daughter nice things to assure her of my love.

In 1994, I met the love of my life, and I married her. A year later, my life changed. I encountered the true and living God, Jesus Christ. I went from serving myself to serving others. The fellowship of others began to speak guidance towards my family. My wife gave birth to my second daughter in 1996. Shortly after, my oldest daughter, then 15 years old, moved into our home. Two years later, we gave birth to our son. Now, the responsibility of marriage and family went to another level.

The changes in my life caused me to learn how to submit. When I say submit, I mean submit to the lordship of Jesus Christ and allow Him to be my guide. Despite life's twists and turns, I stayed on the right track. I had a vision, a purpose and a plan.

As life would have it, my oldest daughter began to display resentment and bitterness. She had a problem seeing me as the loving and committed father that she didn't have. It was something she missed and longed for. In turn, this caused tension in my home. Eventually, she graduated high school and joined the U.S. Air Force.

Several years passed and the relationship between my daughter and I didn't improve. Our contact was like two ships passing in the night. Our conversations were brief. Because of the lack of strength in our relationship, we both felt pain. We both were full of pride and stubbornness. We had settled in our minds that our relationship had no chance of reconciliation.

A father should repent regardless of what he deems he's done right or wrong. I felt that I'd done everything correct and was justified in my actions of sometimes holding my daughter to the wall. Your actions may prompt you to ask yourself, "Is being right better than being alone?" That is a tough question to grapple with. God gave it all for us. On the cross, He said, "Father, forgive them for they do not know what they do." I decided my relationship with my daughter was far more valuable than hurt feelings, acts of disrespect or being right.

During my weekly prayer time, with my prayer accountability partner, God revealed to me that I had the keys to reconcile my relationship with my daughter. At this stage, I'd just about given up hope. But God said, "You repent, make the first move and I will do the rest." One Monday morning, God said, "TEXT HER NOW!" I'm reasoning with God like, "Why? She's not going to call me back, and if she does, what am I going to say?" He said, "JUST DO IT!" Well, I stepped out on a limb. My daughter was no longer speaking to me. She was not accepting or returning my phone calls and text messages. So, I thought, "Okay, here goes nothing." My text read, "Hey please give me a call. I'm no longer interested in bickering with you."

Ten minutes later my phone rang and it was her! When a father repents, reconciliation is sure to follow. I said to my daughter, "I'm sorry I left you at five years old. At that time in my life I wasn't fit to be a father. But, it's no excuse for leaving you. I'm sorry, and I love you very much. Can we make a fresh start?" She replied, "Yes," as we both drowned in tears.

We agreed to breakfast together on the following Saturday morning. I decided that this would be one serious date. I was well prepared for it. I showered and put on fresh clothing and cologne. We met for breakfast and embraced each other with a huge hug. I explained to my daughter, "I feel like I'm on a date with a girl I've always wanted to date, but she never accepted." She finally accepted. To this day, we still have to work on our relationship. But I've committed to do so, because I am the only father she has and I am determined not to repeat the behavior that was modeled to me.

I am convinced, it is not God's will for our lives to be successful in the world's eyes and not show love to our family. Our children are our seed. They are our legacy. We live through them. They did not ask to come into the world and for them, the time we spend with them equates to love.

You will never regret spending time with your children. They grow up fast and the time you spend with them. while they are young, will help them be strong, self-assured and whole. A child's identity is linked to their father. At times it was, and sometimes still is, a bit much. I've grown to embrace the fact that being a public success leaves one empty when one's family is in need.

Mind*Shift* #9: Seek Significance

What would make you significant?

I decree that I am significant
because I am loved by my family.
I make a difference in their lives by living my life
in a manner that brings honor to God.
I take every opportunity to reach out
and let them know that they are loved
by not only me but by God almighty!
In Jesus Name, Amen!

SHIFT 10

EMBRACE YOUR WHY

I am forever grateful for my family. They have been there for me through thick and thin, richer or poorer. They will be with me till death do us part. Over the years, I have drawn strength from them. When the journey got tough, they always encouraged me to keep on pushing. My Mom instilled core family values into all of her children. But there was something so special about our relationship.

> "All that I am, or hope to be, I owe to my angel mother."
> ABRAHAM LINCOLN

Mom was the backbone of our family and the center of our universe. It used to pain me to say it, but at one point in time, my Dad left us to go to California to work with his brother, who built golf courses and to pursue an acting career. My Mom was left with 9 kids to tend to. I don't care what you say, Super Woman couldn't hold a candle to my Mama. For many years, I harbored ill feelings towards my Dad for leaving. It is not until recently that I was able to take a different perspective on his actions. I've come to realize that he was probably at a point where he felt as if life was passing him by. He still had dreams and talent too. When the opportunity presented itself, he mustered up the courage to take a leap of faith, just like I did when I moved to Atlanta. As the saying goes: "Nothing beats a failure but a try." One of my siblings became ill while he was in California and he came back home. He felt his family was more important than an acting career and that was the end of that. Mom welcomed him back with open arms. I guess the old saying, "when you love something, set it free; if it comes back, it's yours, if it doesn't, it never was" is worth mentioning.

When Daddy left, I did not like it. He did, however, work with his brother and sent money home. I wanted him with us. In my mind he left all nine of us. In a sense, I did the same thing. The scripture below is worth remembering. It helps me not to be judgmental.

> "Why do you look at the speck of sawdust in your brother's eye and pay no attention to the plank in your own eye."
> MATTHEW 7:3-5 (KJV)

In other words, we all have things that we have done that are not right. When I was 20, my daughter was born. I did not marry her mother and ended up moving to Atlanta. At the time of her birth, my life was not on the right track. I tried to provide for her and was plagued with guilt for not marrying her mother.

As a parent, you tend to blame yourself for your children's shortcomings. While there has always been a tug in my heart to be a good father to her, I have had to grow into the role. Finally, through much prayer, we have come to the point where we have agreed to walk together.

There are some experiences that you go through, or will go through, in life that will change you forever. While Dad's short departure briefly impacted the family, my Mom's passing changed me forever and shifted my whole way of being. I was truly a "Mama's Boy."

My Mom was diagnosed with pancreatic cancer in February 2017. In April of 2017, she was gone. She never let on how bad she really felt nor how sick she really was. The year prior to her death, she would say – "I know I'm not going to be here much longer." I would just shrug it off, and say: "Aww, Trollie, you're tripping." As I said earlier, Superwoman did not have anything on my Mama. She was a very strong woman. Very rarely did she show any emotion concerning her health. She was always concerned about everyone else.

One day, I got a call at work from my youngest sister, who broke the news to me. She said, "Hey, Mom is really sick -- like for real, for real, sick. Mom has pancreatic cancer." As my heart began to beat rapidly, all I could say was, what?

I immediately called Mom, who was never big on small talk. She answered the phone and said, "Hey Brooks," which is what she called me, "what's up, how are you doing?" I said, "I'm okay, what's up with you? How are you doing? I just heard you were sick." She said, "Yeah that's right. The doctors told me I have pancreatic cancer and it does not look good. I don't have long to live, and I'm okay with that, Brooks; I don't make the cards, I just play the hand I'm dealt! So, when it's my time I'm just going to go on and be with Jesus."

My dear Trollie then shifted the focus off her and asked me how was I doing? I said, "Mom with that info you just gave me I am obviously not doing that great." Silence took over our conversation as I fought back tears. I mustered up the strength to say, "Okay Mom I will see you in a couple days. I Love you! "

I got off the phone, cried and booked flights for my wife and I to visit Mom.

When I arrived home a couple days later, I sat and talked with Mom. We shared memories, laughed in spite of not knowing how long she would be with us. All the way to the end, she never wavered. She stayed the same. One day she said to me, "Son I'm dying." I didn't want to hear her say those words but it was the raw truth.

For the next three weeks, I flew back and forth home to visit Mom; to spend as much time as I could with her. During the first two months, she was still home, upbeat and brutally honest as usual. She was some kind of woman. She never cut corners. She always gave it to you straight. It didn't matter who you were.

I had some great one on one time with her. We made videos. She shared so much with me. I asked Mom questions like, if you could do one thing different in how you raised your nine children, what would that be? Mom was frank she said, "Son, the one thing I would definitely change, is not be so mean. I would have laughed more and taken you all to get cream and not beat your butts so much..." (Mom loved ice cream).

She said to me, "Son, don't be so mean. Learn how to be nice." I said Mom, "How can I not be so mean when that's what you all taught?" She said, "I know, but learn from me, be nice, okay." I said, "I hear you loud and clear." She was so candid, frank and real. I am grateful to have shared many memorable moments with my Mom before her passing.

Mom knew I loved her thin homemade biscuits. I could eat four or five of those things with some of that thick Alaga Syrup, and a huge helping of butter mixed together. I would sop the biscuit in the syrup and butter mixture, which was so thick that it would break the biscuit. That didn't stop me though, I would have syrup dripping down my arm.

One Saturday morning during my visit, Mom got up, sat in a chair and mixed biscuits. She made several pans of biscuits, bacon, sausage and eggs, and my favorite salmon patties. I leaned over and whispered in her ear to say, "Mom thanks for making biscuits this morning, I know you don't feel well."

Mom said, "No problem, son, but you know, this will be the last time I ever make biscuits." It took all I had in me not to crack and break down in tears. She didn't even flinch as she said that; she was tough and true to her love for Jesus Christ.

I left on Sunday and came back the following week. I could see Mom was declining rapidly. We talked a little, she laughed as much as she could. I laid across the bed and talked to her. It was very difficult to watch her health decline so rapidly. As I looked at my Mom, I saw so much gratitude and love on her face, as she just stared into her own world. Her eyes appeared to turn a grayish color and she appeared to be at total peace.

At that moment, I could feel in my heart the end was nearing. Mom didn't want to do much, so as we sat downstairs and talked with family, cousins, nieces and nephews, Mom said, "Hey I'm tired, I'm going to bed." She had to walk upstairs. I said, "Okay Mom, no problem, I will help you." As she began to walk upstairs- I would say about 12 stairs- I asked her if I could help her get upstairs. She said, "Boy, no, I can walk up the stairs on my own." And she did. When she got to the top, she walked into the bedroom and laid across the bed. She said, "Whew, that took all I had." That was Mom, she didn't want anyone to do for her. She was strong-willed and believed she could do it. I guess that's where I get my tenacity from. We are like bulldogs. Why bulldogs? Because their nose is planted upwards so they can breathe while they bite. They don't have a need to let go -- they fight with tenacity.

I flew back to Atlanta on Sunday. I called Mom to let her know I arrived and that I was making biscuits.

I asked her if she wanted me to fix her some, too. I reminded her that it would take me about three hours to fix them. She laughed and said, "Boy, I don't want none of those hard biscuits." Mom and I had an ongoing joke about biscuits. When she taught me how to make them a few years, prior I told her it took me three hours to prepare them. I called her on the phone as I was making them and she said, "Boy how long is it going to take you to fix biscuits? It don't take that long. I showed you how to do it." I said, "Ma, I'm not you, this is hard." She hollered, laughing. I said to her, "Now Mom, when I fix these biscuits for you, although you don't want them, please tell me they are good." Mom said, "Boy I ain't gonna tell you they are good, if they aren't any good." We both chuckled. I said "Mom, I love you." She said, "Son, I love you too!" That was the last conversation I had with my Mom. She died shortly thereafter. Mom told the hospice nurse when the time comes, do not resuscitate.

My Mom was the real deal. She was the rock of our family. She worked from sun up to sun down. She, along with Dad, did the best they could with what they had. I'm forever grateful to God for a mother like mine. Mom and Dad stayed married for 57 years. What a blessing to have parents to care for nine children. They were always there for us. My Mom taught me how to live right and die with dignity. She has always been one of the reasons why I fought so hard to succeed in life. The love in my heart for my Mother and my entire family is eternal. It pushes me to my destiny and helps me to fight for my dream. With their love and God's love, I continue to shift forward.

Mind*Shift* #10: Embrace Your Why

What would you give up your life for?
_____

I decree that as I live my life,
I freely share what God has done for me.
I am compelled to help others
get to the point where they experience
the beauty of God's grace in their lives too.
I will use my unique talents
to draw others unto Him.
And I will use my resources to support
causes that build God's kingdom in the earth.
In Jesus name, Amen!

SHIFT 11

REACH FOR YOUR DESTINY

While growing up in Illinois, I didn't realize, or have a clue, that the things I did in my youth, would have an impact on the course of my life.

> "Destiny is the push of our instincts to the pull of our purpose."
> T.D. JAKES

For as long as I can remember, I had a job. All of us in my household did our part to contribute to running the house. My job was to take out the garbage and of course work the farm during the spring and fall.

When I was about 8, I was able to get a paper route, delivering papers for the Herald News; which I did faithfully for about 6 years. During the winter months, I shoveled snow. Winters in Illinois were brutal. First, I would clean the front of our house and then, I went to my customers in the neighborhood and cleaned their sidewalks, for a fee of-course.

In the summers, when not on the farm, I cut grass. Of course, home first, then I attended to my customers on a bi-weekly bases. I couldn't wait to walk to the gas station, purchase my gas and go make money. What a joy that was. I took pride in what I did, but please note, I collected my money.

I will remember one of my customers until the day I die. She was a lady whose name was Mrs. Doll. She lived on the hill and had a grape vine in her yard. And she didn't mind me eating her grapes while I cut grass. Mrs. Doll always gave me a tip. She would say, "here's a little something extra for you." I think I still remember her because, she always encouraged me to continue what I was doing. She would never forget to tell me what a great job I did. Her compliments, added fuel to my fire and encouraged me to do more and be better. I never missed my appointment to cut her grass.

The times I spent working with my Uncle Jimmie, has proven to have an impact on my destiny. I worked with him on houses-roofing, plumbing, drywalling -every week for several years of my young life. I didn't realize it then, but he was teaching me a strong work ethic. Uncle Jimmie, told me I was a hard worker and he liked the fact that I was consistent. Being a hard worker and being consistent in my work, would propel me forward some 20 plus years down the road.

Who would have imagined that jumping on a roof to tear off shingles, cutting grass, shoveling snow, delivering papers, picking peas, planting greens in the garden, and yes, spending 90 days in a county jail, would make up the fabric of my life, resulting in me becoming an entrepreneur?

One of my favorite poets is Dr. Maya Angelo. She wrote a book titled, *Wouldn't Take Nothing For My Journey*. I tell you, I'm at a place in my life where I really can understand what she meant by that statement. Only God knew that everything I went through would go into making me who I am today.

If I had given up when things were looking down for me, my life really would have been different. I truly believe my life would have been "jacked up" or mediocre for sure.

God used everything that I had been through in Illinois, to help me find my way in Atlanta. It took me many decades to discover that life is about being and becoming who God made me to be. Little did I know, when I was a little boy, I was learning how to become an entrepreneur.

Although I had to work odd jobs, when I first moved to Atlanta, my work ethic, belief that better was before me, and God was for me, was what sustained me.

I have not always done what's right and still miss the mark on occasion. But one of the best things I've ever done was to decide to accept Jesus as my Lord and Savior and build a relationship with Him.

When I did that, I received a grace upon my life that turned me and my life around for the better. I went from not having a pay check, to living from pay check to pay check, to not having to check whether or not I have enough in the bank to cover a check.

God's grace has enabled me to go from a borrower to a lender. God's grace is merely how He extends goodness to us despite what we have done or what we are doing. Grace is favor from Him that we did not earn. It is the help and strength we receive from God through His son Christ Jesus. As we build a relationship with Christ, we are able to understand the implication of His grace upon our lives.

Many years of my life were spent making up for my past mistakes and making money to acquire the finer things in life. Now that I have more years behind me than in front of me – I am compelled to use my resources to make a difference in the lives of others.

When we reach the point of being successful, value is added to ourselves. Primarily, this entails acquiring finances to enhance our lifestyle with life's luxury items. But when we realize the source of our success – we're driven to care more than just about ourselves. I'm sure you would agree that it's considered a blessing to be successful. I was always taught that we are blessed to be a blessing. When we are a blessing to others, we begin to care about making a difference in the lives of others. The more we demonstrate that we care about others with our time and resources - we shift from success to significance. I have been on this earth quite a few decades and can honestly say, there is no greater feeling than being able to give someone something and not expect anything in return.

I believe your destiny will take you to a place where God has need of you to fulfill your purpose and calling. You can plan your way, BUT, know that God orders your steps!

Today, I embrace the fact that my mission, my calling, my assignment, is to uplift and encourage those that have been broken and lost hope. I am called to give young and old, men and women, hope and purpose, regardless of their past mistakes, failures, education level or environment. Shift your mindset to believe there is hope- YES YOU CAN! and YES YOU WILL! - if you only believe!

God has a purpose and reason for your life. Your experiences prepare you for your life's journey. He uses everything that you go through to help someone else along their way. In essence, God uses us to make a difference in the lives of others, with the talents, gifts and abilities that is given to us.

Whatever good is in your heart to do, put your trust in God and believe that you can do it. When you start out, you might not know exactly how everything will come together, but I promise, God will send the resources you need to complete the task, providing it is His will for your life. And if it is His will, it will involve you using what you have been blessed with to help others

It is within you to know why God made you. Those things that you are drawn to are not accidental.

> For I know the plans I have for you, declares the Lord, plans to prosper you and not to harm you, plans to give you hope and a future.
> **JEREMIAH 29:11 (NIV)**

Mind*Shift* #11: Reach for Your Destiny

*If you could write your future,
who or what would you be or become?*

I decree that I am committed to believing
that nothing is impossible with God.
It is written in the Bible that
He knew me before I was formed in my mother's womb
and has plans to prosper me.
His plans for my life are great
and I will look into my heart to pursue them.
In Jesus name, Amen!

The Amos Shift

SHIFT 12

LEAVE A LEGACY

At one point I used to think leaving a legacy was about having a building with your name on it. I thought legacy was associated with rich people or famous people. Actually, legacy is more about love than anything else.

> "Please think about your legacy because you are writing it every day."
> GARY VAYNERCHUK

As you continue to build your legacy, be sure to regularly ask God what He wants to be for you -in your present situation -that He could not have been at any other time in your life?

It is not my intention to misguide you into thinking that when you surrender your life to God everything will be all right. Trials are a part of life. But walking with God is the best decision you will ever make. My worst days with Him, does not compare to my best days without Him.

Sometimes, the things that we go through, that we consider bad, turn out to be used for good in God's kingdom. God can take our mess and give us a message. He can take the test we go through in life and give us a testimony. When we are able to go through something difficult and use our experience to help others – we, in turn are leaving a legacy in the hearts of others.

Recently, I was faced with a challenge. Because of my faith, I was able to experience victory. Like most men, going to the doctor for an annual exam was not something that I delighted in doing. As a matter of fact, for many years of my life, I put off going to the doctor and even self-diagnosed myself. Going to the doctor's office once a year to get blood work and a prostate check was mentally exhausting. At one point, I decided that I don't care, I'm not going to the doctor and get another prostate exam.

Then the Lord spoke to me clearly and said, "You old, selfish thing. You can only think about yourself; you have a family that you lead, provide for and protect. I have made you a Priest and King of your family. What happens to your family if you leave this earth sooner than expected?"

At that point, I got the message, and fully understood, that simple diseases are preventable. I started to visit my healthcare provider regularly, because early detection is the key to long life. As men, we have an obligation to take care of ourselves. I heard a quote once that said, "An ounce of prevention is worth a pound of cure."

Yes, men that means going to see your doctor once a year, especially when you reach your forties. That old prostate cancer check is necessary, even though it feels like a major violation of your manhood. The old dreaded elbows on the table and "this won't hurt a bit," is unavoidable. Let the truth be known, a day later, I'm still in the bed crying about what just happened in that doctor's office. It definitely isn't a pretty thing. But it's actually lifesaving.

What do you do when you have taken good care of yourself, visited the doctor for your regular physical, and the doctor says, your prostate numbers are elevated? He continues with, we need to keep our eyes on your numbers, they are not normal, Well, a couple months later, my prostate-specific antigen, PSA numbers, were elevated and the doctor said that I needed to have a biopsy. What? A biopsy? I went to the doctor's office to have a biopsy done. While waiting on the results, I found myself praying and asking God for no negative results. I was not really afraid, but kind of concerned in a crazy sort of way. The results came back. My doctor called and said that I needed to come into the office to discuss the results. At that point, I stared to worry. I kept asking myself, what is he going to say?

His response was, 'it's treatable and it's very early." But we need to decide about how we will proceed. He said, "You have three options. One, we can surgically cut it out. Two, we can opt for permanent radioactive seed implants which are a form of radiation therapy for prostate cancer. The implants remain in place permanently, and become biologically inert (inactive) after about 10 months. This technique allows a high dose of radiation to be delivered to the prostate with limited damage to surrounding tissues. Lastly, you can opt for Cryotherapy which is a "cold therapy." Cryotherapy is a procedure used to destroy tissue of both benign and malignant lesions by the freezing and re-thawing process.

Upon processing what he said, I asked him, "What do you recommend? He said, "I recommend you take it out and let's schedule it for next month." What? By now, I'm floored by his answer. The only thing I heard was, I wouldn't be able to be intimate with my wife. I said to him, "You mean I can't, I can't put in that work with my wife?" I said to myself, I'm still relatively young you know! I'm married, it's legal for us to have sex. I said, "Doc are you telling me no more sex? My doctor chuckled and said, "No you will be fine in that area." You have no idea how happy I was to hear those words. WHEW!!

I said to the doctor, "Let me go home, do my research and I will get back to you in a couple weeks." I researched and researched. I visited three other doctors in Atlanta. All the while, my wife is saying, "Just let them cut out the cancer, like they recommended doing."

I was still apprehensive and continued to talk and ask people who have gone through this experience. I wasn't aware that there were so many men who have gone through this deadly disease and survived.

After doing my research, and of course praying, I was led to MD Anderson Center in Houston Texas. I was told that I would be down for a couple weeks while the seeds take affect and then I would be back up and running as normal. My wife asked me, "Why are we going way down there? You have no support system it's so far away." I told her, "I'm going to find the best possible care." I found a doctor who was the best and he had my solution. I was led to MD Anderson Center to get the seed implants, a simple surgery. I had to go to Texas for a consultation. I met with the doctor's assistant who informed me that after running several tests, I was a great candidate for seed implants! His words were music to my ears, as I had to wait a little longer to see the doctor. At the time, I was rushing trying to get out of the doctor's office, because I had a plane to catch. I had been in the doctor's office taking test all day and I just wanted to get on a plane and go home.

My primary doctor couldn't see me at the moment unless I wanted to wait. If I waited, I could miss my flight back to Atlanta. Fortunately, my primary doctor walked in shortly thereafter, and said, "Hello, how are you?" I said, "I'm fine." He says, "Well, elbows on the table and drop your pants." I'm like, "NO, NOT AGAIN, your assistant just did this. Why do I need to do it again? OMG not again, twice in one day, really?" I said to myself this is why men refuse to go to the doctor.

Then the doctor violates me once again. He said it again, "Elbows on the table, pants down." Dayum! Can I say that as a Christian? WELL DAYUM! The doctor pops his glove and gives me the blues. He looks at the results from the MRI, the same results his assistant looked at and said well, "I'm not sure if I will recommend the seed implants. I know that's what you want but that's not what I recommend." I'm like well, "What do you recommend? He said, "I recommend you come back and do another MRI with the mars camera."

I'm like, "Okay cool." I scheduled another appointment two weeks later for the exam. I never, in all my days, knew an MRI would be so intense. Afterwards, my wife and I flew back to Atlanta. I said to Von, "Well whatever this doctor says for me to do that's what I'm going to do."

Two weeks later, we head back to Texas for intense x-rays, which lasted one hour and fifteen minutes in an MRI tube. My knees up and strapped in with a camera up my john brown hind parts. I never dreamed this could be happening to me. The nurse said that they had men just run out and say no I'm not doing it. I was almost at that point, but something in me said don't be selfish.

The results were immediate. We went down stairs to my doctor and he said, I recommend you do the surgery. I still wasn't sold on having the surgery. My doctor sent me to another doctor on campus. The second doctor tells me the same thing. I still wasn't sold and finally the doctor said, okay this is what you do, go home, get a urinalysis to determine how well you urinate.

I came back to Atlanta and the urine study results looked really good, appearing to work in my favor.

The doctor's office sent the results back to MD Anderson. We flew back to Texas, my doctor looks at the results and said, no the implants are not going to work, your prostate is too large for seeds.

He said, if you still want the seeds, we can do a surgical procedure that they call a Roto Rooter. Come back in six months, we will see how it looks and then determine if you are eligible for the seed implants. I decided to go through with it, which was one of the most difficult decisions that I've ever made in my entire life.

However, I ended up seeing another doctor on campus. At that point, it was obvious that all three doctors had collaborated and determined the way my body was made, seed implants would not be the best route. This doctor told me that he was looking out for my long-term health and quality of life.

Finally, I accepted the fact. I told my wife, "Okay, looks like surgery, no roto rooter procedure. I'm not going through two surgeries just to determine if I am eligible for seed implants." Besides, roto rooter reminded me too much of a plumber and I was not a sink or a toilet.

My surgery was scheduled one month later. I was told that the robotic surgery procedure lasts 12-16 hours. I was reassured that I was a great candidate for that type of procedure and it would probably only take 8 hours. I loved the doctors' attitude. He was definitely good at what he does. I had one major concern. I told the doctor, "Please don't cut the vein that destroys my baby making abilities!

ALL YOU MEN KNOW WHAT I MEAN!"

The doctor said, "I got you--no worries. I'm the best in the business, you came for the best, you got the best." After 8 hours of surgery -- all went well. I stayed in a hotel for one week with my wife. During my recuperation, I am thankful for my brother Paul for holding down the business. Two of my dear friends, Lamonte and Mike, flew to Texas to hang out with me for a few days which really made me feel good. There is something to be said about being a friend during a time of need.

I have decided to never let my cancer go to waste. The experience I had, I will tell the world how good and awesome God is. If I had never had the experience, my sensitivity to cancer patients would not be what it is today. I'm grateful that I'm three years healed and cancer free. Early detection is the key to longevity. No cancer! Cancer free and going strong in more ways than one, if you know what I mean.

Exercising and eating a proper diet is key to longevity. Now that I've gotten older, I exercise three to four days a week and eat well. I visit my doctor on a regular basis and make sure I have a full physical annually. If I sense something isn't right, I consult with my physician immediately.

Looking back on this whole ordeal is bitter sweet, as I learned a great deal through the experience. First and foremost, whatever you're going through – always, always, talk to God about it. God answers prayer and prayer changes things or it will change something in you that will give you a calmness to deal with whatever comes your way.

Mind*Shift* #12: Leave a Legacy

Your Life Line

Fill in the boxes and draw a vertical line marking where you are in your life.

| Date of Birth | | Age of Death |

Example

1970   89

(This exercise will help you see just how much time you have to leave a mark in the earth!)

I decree that my legacy reflects love.
Others will say that they are a better person because of me.
I impart inspiration, knowledge and wisdom
in the hearts and minds of others.
I am honest. I have integrity.
My strong character will reverberate in the earth
for generations to come.
In Jesus name, Amen!

EPILOGUE

God desires to bless you more than you could ever imagine. He loves you more than you could imagine and your family loves you too. They might not be able to articulate it the way you need to hear it, but none the less – they love you. They might not have done things the way you think they should have. Or they might have done things that they should not have done. Notwithstanding, they are your family. The more you learn about them, particularly your parents, especially during their younger years – the better you're able to understand who they are and why they did or didn't do certain things.

When we can stop being judgmental about what someone did or didn't do for us – we're able to move past our hurts, hang-ups and habits. Our experiences in life molds us into who we are today. Sometimes our life experiences have an adverse effect on who we become. I have known many people whose parents were not the best, but they managed to rise up from mediocrity. They used their situation as a car uses fuel to go. They made up their minds not to be like the one or the ones who were supposed to care for them. Conversely, I know people who had an ideal upbringing who choose to live a life of mediocrity.

We all need to be loved and made to feel special. Sometimes we're able to get the love we need and the way we need it from our family. And sometimes our need is so great, only God can fill the void. It is said, the two most important days in your life are the day you are born and the day you figure out why.

I really believe that there's another important day in our life. I believe it is more important than the other two. It is they day we accept Jesus Christ as our Lord and Savior. Accepting Christ is different for each of us.

For me, one day I was in my apartment and had a visit from God. That visit prompted me to change my ways. I no longer had a desire for alcohol, clubbing and my partying it up lifestyle. When my wife returned home from one of her trips, I told her I'm giving up drinking. She was shocked and dismayed. When I look back, I can't help but thank God. At that point in my life my priorities became: God first, family second, then career/business.

Did I still have challenges to overcome? Absolutely! Putting God first enables me to live my life in a manner that brings Him glory and in so doing – my life is far richer than I ever imagined and more meaningful than I ever dreamed possible.

As you continue to forgive others -- especially yourself-- and put God first, amazing things will begin to unfold in your life. Putting God first is about working on your relationship with Him. And in order to know Him – it requires that you study His word – the Bible. Notice I said relationship and not religion. Religion is a set of rules that must be followed in order to be considered a Christian or to get into Heaven. A relationship with God is when you recognize that He is your father, friend and judge. It's when you believe in your heart that there isn't anything you have done, doing, or will do, to make Him love you any more or less than He already does.

You see, God sent His son Jesus into the world to die for our sins. Therefore, when He looks at us, He looks at us through the eyes of Christ.

When you admit that you are a sinner, believe that Jesus died for you and chose to accept you and that you have accepted Him as your Lord and Savior – He takes residence inside of you. You then have a prophet, priest and king on the inside.

People will show up and be a blessing. Opportunities that you might not necessarily be qualified for will open up. You will begin to experience what it means to be blessed. Shifts will occur in your life that move you to where you want to be.

You are a child of God, made in His image. Taking time to read His word and associate with people who do the same will help you to become a son of God.

As you continue to grow, remember that the best is yet to come. God is in the business of miracles. He will make allowances for anything you think you have lost. Raise your expectancy and be open to the possibilities that lie ahead for you. I will leave you with a word from the Prophet Amos, for you to hold onto as you shift to your next phase in life.

MY DECREE FOR YOU!

I decree that all you hoped to be will be revealed to you and in the earth. That you will consider it an honor to put God first. That from this day forward you will believe more in Him and yourself. And you will see your life shift to reflect the results of the phenomenal plan for your life that God put in your heart!

Your Brother in Christ!
George

Fashions

Featuring a wide range of clothing and accessories for men and women!

Designed for fit. Loved for style!

www.jagwearfashion.com

www.ingramcontent.com/pod-product-compliance
Lightning Source LLC
Chambersburg PA
CBHW070437010526
44118CB00014B/2080

www.ingramcontent.com/pod-product-compliance
Lightning Source LLC
Chambersburg PA
CBHW070428010526
44118CB00014B/1952